20 ^{take} minutes!

20 take minutes!

Chef
express

Published by:
TRIDENT REFERENCE PUBLISHING
801 12th Avenue South, Suite 400
Naples, Fl 34102 USA

Tel: + 1 (239) 649-7077
www.tridentreference.com
email: sales@tridentreference.com

Take 20 Minutes!
© TRIDENT REFERENCE PUBLISHING

Publisher
Simon St. John Bailey

Editor-in-chief
Susan Knightley

Prepress
Precision Prep & Press

Includes Index
ISBN 1582796807
UPC 6 15269 96807 9

Printed in The United States

introduction

The pleasure of good eating comes from many things. Good ingredients, enjoyable company, reliable recipes –and, of course, enough time to get everything cooked and on to the table.

For many of us time is the element that's hardest to find. We all seem to be in a constant hurry these days.

There's work, children, shopping, keeping the house in order. Often, last of all these priorities, comes the time to cook and enjoy mealtimes together.

What can be done to help? The answer: discover quick and easy ways to cook meals everyone can enjoy. That's where this book comes in.

Every recipe has been carefully timed to help you. They clock in 20 minutes or less from start to finish, and produce good "real" food that tastes delicious.

The best thing about this book is that it puts you first. The recipes will allow you to fit in all the important things in your life –family, friends and work– and still make it possible for you to bring nice meals to the table.

All with minimum fuss and in the shortest possible time.

Time saving

As so often in the kitchen, it helps to plan ahead. A well-stocked store cupboard is a great help to speed your cooking. Check your inventory of canned food as cans are highly practical for an infinite number of recipes. The same may be said for your freezer. It is useful to have frozen ground meat, vegetables, pastries, bread and cooked rice and pasta, that can be quickly reheated in the microwave.

Being organized and assembling all your ingredients and equipment before you start will save you time in cooking and cleaning up. First of all, look at the recipe and read through the method. Then, following the ingredients listing, collect and prepare the foods you will require, then you will have them to hand when you start cooking. The ingredients are always listed in their order of use. The next step is to go through the method and get out the equipment that you will need. You should also check the recipe at this stage to see if the oven will be used and, if so, turn it on to preheat.

Now, you just have to start cooking to confirm that the preparation of a meal in 20 minutes is possible and rewarding.

Difficulty scale

■□□| Easy to do

■■□| Requires attention

■■■| Requires experience

cold
beetroot soup

■□□ I Cooking time: 0 minute - Preparation time: 5 minutes

method

1. Make sure beets and yogurt are thoroughly chilled.
2. Purée beets with their juice and pepper in a blender or food processor until smooth. You may need to add a little water if consistency is too thick.
3. Serve with a spoonful of yogurt on top. Garnish with parsley sprig.

ingredients

> **870 g/1³/4 lb canned baby beets, undrained**
> **1 teaspoon cracked black peppercorns**
> **¹/4 cup natural yogurt**
> **parsley for garnish**

....
Serves 4

tip from the chef

Yogurt can be replaced by cream cheese or lightly whipped cream.

soup with meatballs

■□□ | Cooking time: 15 minutes - Preparation time: 5 minutes

method

1. In a large saucepan boil wine over high heat until reduced by half. Reduce heat to medium and add stock, tomatoes, onion and tomato paste (a). Bring to the boil, reduce heat and simmer for 1 minute.
2. Roll sausage mince into small balls, place carefully into the simmering soup (b) and cook for 7 minutes.
3. Add mushrooms, pimentos and spinach (c), cook for a further 3 minutes. Serve hot.

....
Serves 4

ingredients

> 1 cup dry white wine
> 3¹/₂ cups chicken stock
> 1 cup canned tomatoes, chopped
> 1 onion, sliced
> 2 tablespoons tomato paste (purée)
> 350 g/11 oz sausage mince
> 100 g/3¹/₂ oz large mushrooms, sliced
> 2 pimentos, drained and cut into thin slices
> 1 cup chopped spinach

tip from the chef

This soup results even more tasty if it is served with country bread toasts.

a   b   c

beggar's soup

■□□ I Cooking time: 15 minutes - Preparation time: 5 minutes

method

1. Toast bread slices on both sides and rub it with garlic.
2. Bring chicken stock to the boil, add broccoli and cook for 30 seconds.
3. Ladle soup into warmed soup bowls, place two or three pieces of garlic toast in each bowl and sprinkle with Parmesan cheese.

ingredients

> **1 French bread stick, cut into thin slices**
> **1 clove garlic, halved**
> **4 cups chicken stock**
> **1 cup broccoli**
> **1/2 cup grated Parmesan cheese**

....

Serves 4

tip from the chef

A good idea for winter: serve soup in ramekins and place under the grill until cheese melts.

tofu
and broccoli salad

■□□ | Cooking time: 3 minutes - Preparation time: 5 minutes

ingredients

> 2¹/2 cups broccoli flowerets
> 200 g/6¹/2 oz tofu, cut into 2 cm/³/4 in cubes
> 1 red pepper, seeded and cut into 1 cm/¹/2 in squares
> 3 tablespoons smooth peanut butter
> ¹/2 cup cream
> 3 tablespoons water

method

1. Bring a large saucepan of water to the boil, add broccoli and cook for 1 minute. Remove broccoli with a slotted spoon and refresh under cold water.
2. Arrange broccoli, tofu and pepper on serving plate.
3. Heat peanut butter in a medium saucepan over low heat. Stir in half the cream until combined. Remove from heat, stir in remaining cream and water.
4. Pour sauce over salad and serve immediately.

....
Serves 4

tip from the chef

Tofu, also known as soy bean curd, is a soft, cheese-like food made by curdling fresh hot soy milk with a coagulant.

chicken
and pineapple salad

■☐☐ | Cooking time: 0 minute - Preparation time: 5 minutes

method

1. Arrange watercress, chicken pieces, pineapple, walnuts and tomatoes on serving plate.
2. Pour over combined French dressing and curry powder.

....
Serves 4

ingredients

> **2 cups watercress sprigs**
> **1 cooked chicken, bones and skin removed, meat torn into pieces**
> **1 cup canned pineapple pieces, drained**
> **1/2 cup walnut halves**
> **1/2 cup cherry tomatoes, halved**
> **1/4 cup French dressing**
> **2 teaspoons mild curry powder**

tip from the chef

To make French dressing, blend or process 1/3 cup vinegar, 1 egg, 1 tablespoon sugar and 1 tablespoon paprika with salt and pepper to taste. With machine running add 1 tablespoon oil.

salad niçoise

■ □ □ | Cooking time: 0 minute - Preparation time: 15 minutes

ingredients

> 1 lettuce of your choice, leaves separated
> 500 g/1 lb fresh young broad beans, shelled
> 1 large red pepper, cut into thin strips
> marinated artichoke hearts, halved
> 250 g/8 oz cherry tomatoes
> 1 large cucumber, cut into strips
> 3 spring onions, chopped
> 12 canned anchovy fillets, drained
> 250 g/8 oz canned tuna in water, drained
> 185 g/6 oz marinated black olives
> 6 hard boiled eggs, quartered
> 1/4 cup/60 ml/2 fl oz olive oil
> freshly ground black pepper

method

1. Arrange lettuce leaves on a large serving platter or in a large salad bowl.
2. Top with beans, red pepper, artichokes, tomatoes, cucumber, spring onions, anchovy fillets, tuna, olives and eggs.
3. Drizzle with oil and season to taste with black pepper.

....

Serves 4-6

tip from the chef

This is an easy spring or summer dish. As the broad beans are eaten raw it must be made with very fresh young beans. It should be noted that there are many versions of this salad and that the traditional salad does not include potatoes or other cooked vegetables.

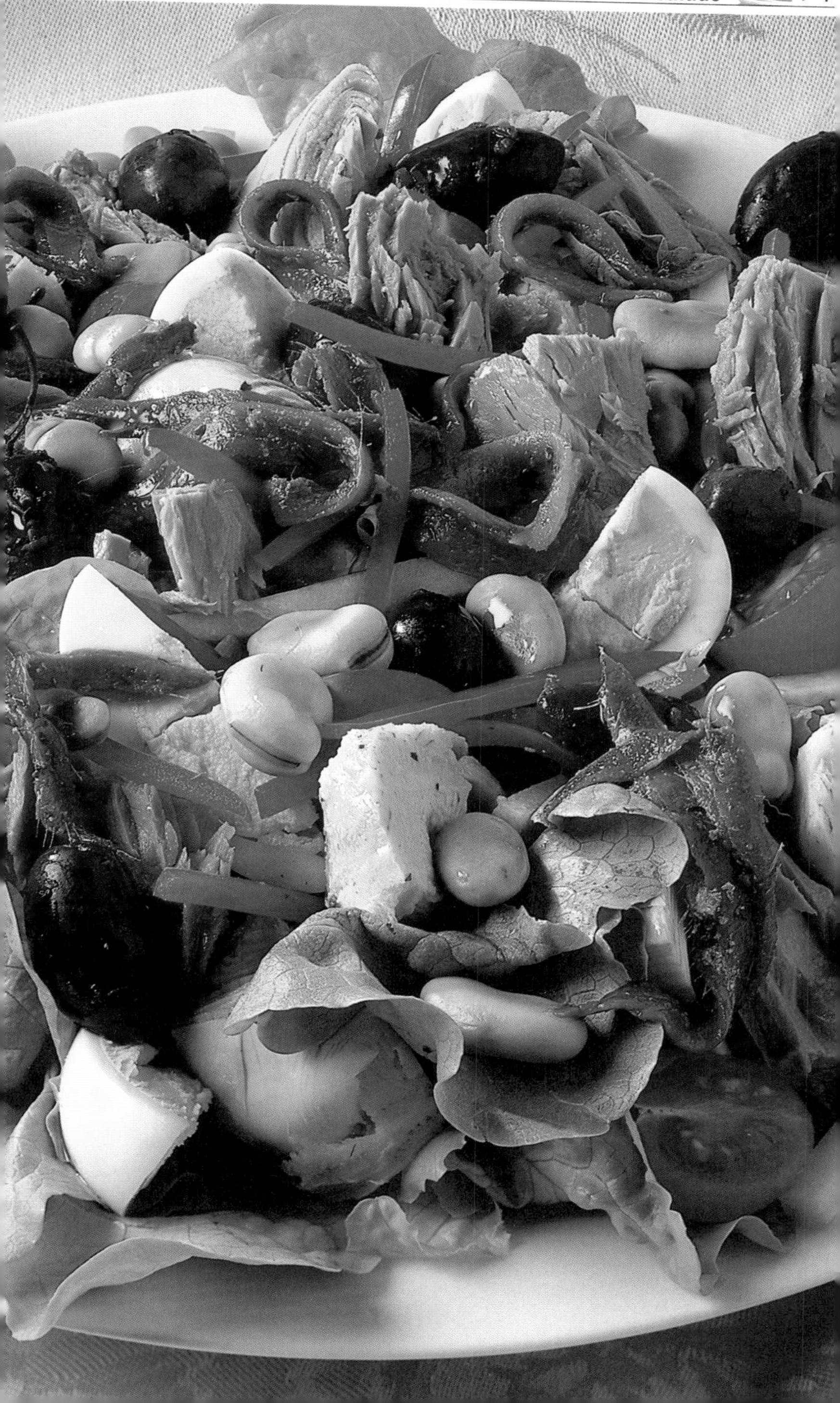

white
cheese dip

open
sandwiches

■□□ | Cooking time: 5 minutes - Preparation time: 15 minutes

ingredients

pimento and cheese

> 250 g/1/2 lb ricotta cheese
> 1/2 cup grated Parmesan cheese
> 1 tablespoon chopped chives
> 4 thick slices of wholemeal bread
> 4 slices of pimento, drained
> 1 red onion, thinly sliced
> parsley to garnish

chicken and avocado

> 4 slices bread
> 50 g/13/4 oz cream cheese, softened
> 4 tablespoons mayonnaise
> 2 cups cooked chicken, bones and skin removed, meat torn into pieces
> 4 slices mature Cheddar cheese
> 1 avocado, peeled, seeded and quartered
> 1 tablespoon chopped chives

method

1. To make pimento and cheese sandwiches, combine ricotta cheese, Parmesan cheese and chives in a small bowl, mix well. Spread each slice of bread with ricotta cheese mixture, top with pimento and onion rings, garnish with parsley sprigs.

2. To make chicken and avocado sandwiches, spread each slice of bread with cream cheese, then with mayonnaise. Top with some chicken and a slice of cheese and grill until cheese has melted. Remove from grill, place avocado on top and sprinkle with chives.

....
Serves 4 each

tip from the chef

To inhibit the avocado from going dark, it is convenient to cut it just before serving.
If you need to cut it in advance, drizzle with lemon juice.

salmon
and egg sandwiches

avocado
with seafood

■□□ | Cooking time: 0 minute - Preparation time: 10 minutes

method

1. Cut avocados in half and remove stones. Scoop out the flesh carefully, reserving skins.
2. Blend or process avocado flesh with lemon juice, sour cream, mayonnaise and cayenne pepper; purée until smooth. Stir in prawns.
3. Spoon mixture into avocado skins. Garnish with parsley and lemon slices.

....
Serves 4

ingredients

> **2 ripe avocados**
> **1 tablespoon freshly squeezed lemon juice**
> **$1/4$ cup sour cream**
> **3 tablespoons mayonnaise**
> **$1/4$ teaspoon cayenne pepper**
> **155 g/5 oz cooked prawns, shelled and deveined**
> **1 tablespoon finely chopped parsley**
> **8 lemon slices**

tip from the chef

If you wish to enrich this recipe, add a touch of ketchup to the processed mixture and add sliced hearts of palm along with the shrimp.

rosetta
pizzas

◼☐☐ I Cooking time: 10 minutes - Preparation time: 5 minutes

method

1. Spread each half roll with tomato purée, top with prosciutto, then mozzarella cheese, red pepper and parsley.
2. Bake in a moderate oven for 10 minutes or until cheese melts.

Serves 4

ingredients

> 2 rosetta rolls, halved
> 3 tablespoons tomato purée
> 8 slices prosciutto
> 4 thin slices mozzarella cheese
> 2 tablespoons red pepper, seeded and finely chopped
> 2 tablespoons chopped parsley

tip from the chef

Once out of the oven, spray with olive oil and sprinkle some chopped basil to add freshness and fragrance.

vermicelli with
broccoli and almonds

■□□ | Cooking time: 15 minutes - Preparation time: 5 minutes

ingredients

> **2 cups broccoli flowerets**
> **4 tablespoons butter**
> **2 tablespoons chopped spring onions**
> **2 cloves garlic, crushed**
> **1 teaspoon sambal oelek (chili paste)**
> **1/2 teaspoon cracked black pepper**
> **1/2 cup chopped blanched almonds**
> **3 tablespoons white wine**
> **3 tablespoons olive oil**
> **500 g/1 lb vermicelli**

method

1. Blanch broccoli in a saucepan of boiling water for 2 minutes. Drain, refresh under cold water, drain again and set aside.

2. Melt butter in a large frying pan over moderate heat, add spring onions, garlic, sambal oelek, pepper and almonds, cook for 2 minutes. Add wine and oil, cook for a further 3 minutes, then add blanched broccoli and heat through.

3. Cook vermicelli in a large saucepan of boiling water until al dente, drain and toss with broccoli mixture.

....
Serves 4

tip from the chef

Sambal oelek is made of chilies, with no other additives such as garlic or spices for a much simpler taste.

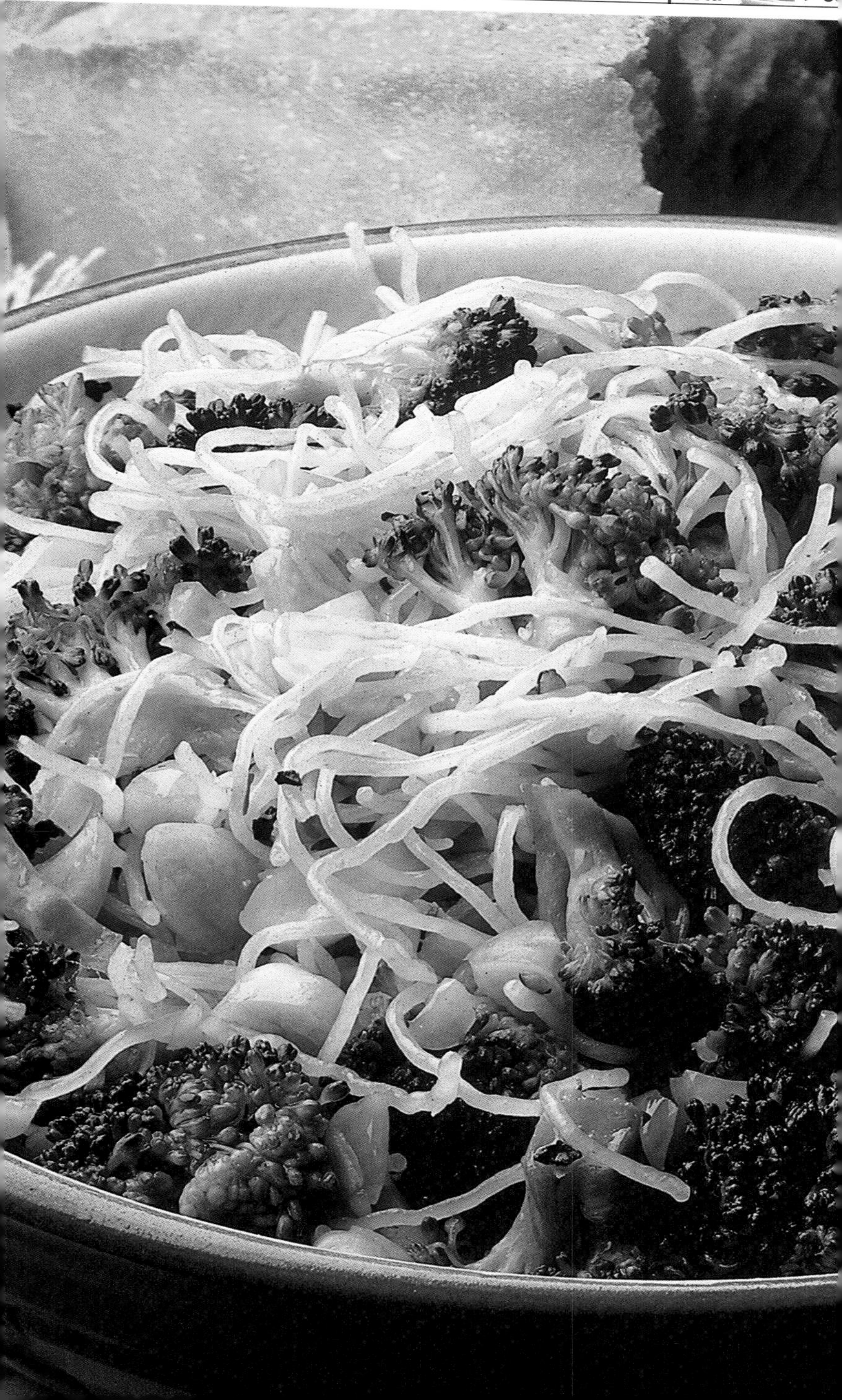

fettuccine
with scallops

■■□ | Cooking time: 15 minutes - Preparation time: 5 minutes

method

1. Bring a large saucepan of water to the boil, add fettuccine and cook until just tender.
2. Meanwhile, melt butter in a large frying pan over moderate heat. Add red pepper and spring onions, cook for 1 minute. Add cream, bring to the boil, reduce heat and simmer for 3-5 minutes or until cream begins to thicken. Add scallops and black pepper, cook until scallops are opaque, about 1 minute.
3. Drain fettuccine and pour scallop sauce over the top, sprinkle with parsley.

....
Serves 4

ingredients

> **500 g/1 lb fettuccine**
> **30 g/1 oz butter**
> **1 red pepper, seeded, cut into strips**
> **2 tablespoons chopped spring onions**
> **1 1/2 cups cream**
> **500 g/1 lb scallops**
> **1/2 teaspoon ground black pepper**
> **1 tablespoon chopped fresh parsley**

tip from the chef

Always take care not to overcook the scallops because they toughen easily.

linguine
with prawns

■■□ | Cooking time: 15 minutes - Preparation time: 5 minutes

ingredients

> **500 g/1 lb linguine**
> **4 tablespoons butter**
> **2 cloves garlic, crushed**
> **1 large onion, chopped**
> **3 tablespoons pitted and chopped black olives**
> **2 cups canned tomatoes, undrained**
> **1 teaspoon sugar**
> **1 tablespoon tomato paste (purée)**
> **2 teaspoons dried rosemary, chopped**
> **315 g/10 oz medium uncooked prawns, shelled and deveined, tails left intact**
> **1/4 cup freshly grated Parmesan cheese**
> **2 tablespoons finely chopped fresh parsley**

method

1. Bring a large saucepan of water to the boil, add linguine and cook until just tender, drain, set aside.
2. Melt butter in a large frying pan over moderate heat. Add garlic, onion and olives, cook for 3 minutes, stirring constantly.
3. Add tomatoes and their juice, sugar, tomato paste and rosemary, cook for a further 5 minutes. Add prawns and cook for a further 3 minutes.
4. Add linguine to the sauce and toss well. Serve with Parmesan cheese and parsley.

....
Serves 4

tip from the chef

If you cannot get raw prawns, use the ones that come already cooked and add to the sauce along with the pasta.

fish with
green aioli

■□□ | Cooking time: 5 minutes - Preparation time: 10 minutes

method

1. Melt butter in a large frying pan over moderate heat, add garlic, cook for 1 minute. Add fish pieces and cook for 2 minutes each side or until cooked through.

2. Meanwhile, to make aioli, place egg yolks, parsley, basil, chives, lemon juice and garlic in a blender or food processor. While motor is operating, gradually add oil, drop by drop, until aioli reaches a suitable consistency.

3. Arrange watercress and fish pieces on a serving plate, pour aioli over the top.

....
Serves 4

ingredients

> **3 tablespoons butter**
> **1 clove garlic, crushed**
> **440 g/14 oz bream fillets, cut into 2 cm/3/4 in squares**
> **2 cups watercress sprigs**

green aioli

> **3 egg yolks**
> **1/2 cup chopped parsley**
> **1/2 cup chopped basil**
> **1/4 cup chopped chives**
> **2 tablespoons freshly squeezed lemon juice**
> **1 clove garlic, crushed**
> **1 cup oil**

tip from the chef

It is important not to overcook the fish, in order to not upset its texture.

fish with brandy sauce

■■□ | Cooking time: 10 minutes - Preparation time: 5 minutes

ingredients
> **1 tablespoon butter**
> **4 fish fillets, 200 g/ 6¹/₂ oz each**
> **4 tablespoons brandy**
> **²/₃ cup sour cream**
> **²/₃ cup cream**
> **3 tablespoons freshly squeezed orange juice**
> **4 tablespoons chopped roasted pistachios**
> **shredded orange rind for garnish**

method
1. Heat butter in a large frying pan over moderate heat. Add fish fillets and cook for 3 minutes each side or until just cooked. Set aside in a warm oven.
2. Add brandy, sour cream, cream and orange juice to pan, cook until sauce is reduced by half.
3. Spoon sauce over fish fillets, sprinkle pistachios on top and garnish with shredded orange rind.

....
Serves 4

tip from the chef
This delicate fish recipe is ideal for entertaining without spuding much time in the kitchen.

salmon
with orange butter

ginger honey chicken wings

■■□ | Cooking time: 10 minutes - Preparation time: 10 minutes

method

1. Lightly dust veal fillets with flour.
2. Melt butter in a large frying pan over moderate heat. Add garlic and cook for 1 minute. Add wine and cook for a further 1 minute.
3. Add sage and fillets, cook for 2 minutes each side or until just cooked. Serve immediately with blanched vegetables if desired.

ingredients

> **8 medium veal fillets**
> **1/4 cup plain flour**
> **3 tablespoons butter**
> **2 cloves garlic, crushed**
> **3 tablespoons wine**
> **2 tablespoons chopped fresh sage**

....
Serves 4

tip from the chef

To give a different flavor to this exquisite dish, substitute rosemary or thyme for sage.

lamb chops
with mint pesto

■ ■ □ | Cooking time: 10 minutes - Preparation time: 5 minutes

ingredients
- > **8 lamb chops**
- > **2 cloves garlic, chopped**
- > **1/2 cup mint leaves**
- > **1/4 cup parsley leaves**
- > **1/3 cup chopped walnut halves**
- > **1/4 teaspoon black pepper**
- > **1/3 cup olive oil**

method
1. Skewer each chop to hold neatly in place. Grill chops until cooked through, about 4 minutes each side.
2. Meanwhile, place garlic, mint, parsley, walnuts and pepper in a food processor and pulse until just chopped, pouring in oil in a thin stream.
3. Serve chops with mint pesto.

....
Serves 4

tip from the chef
Serve with baked vegetables and you will have a complete meal.

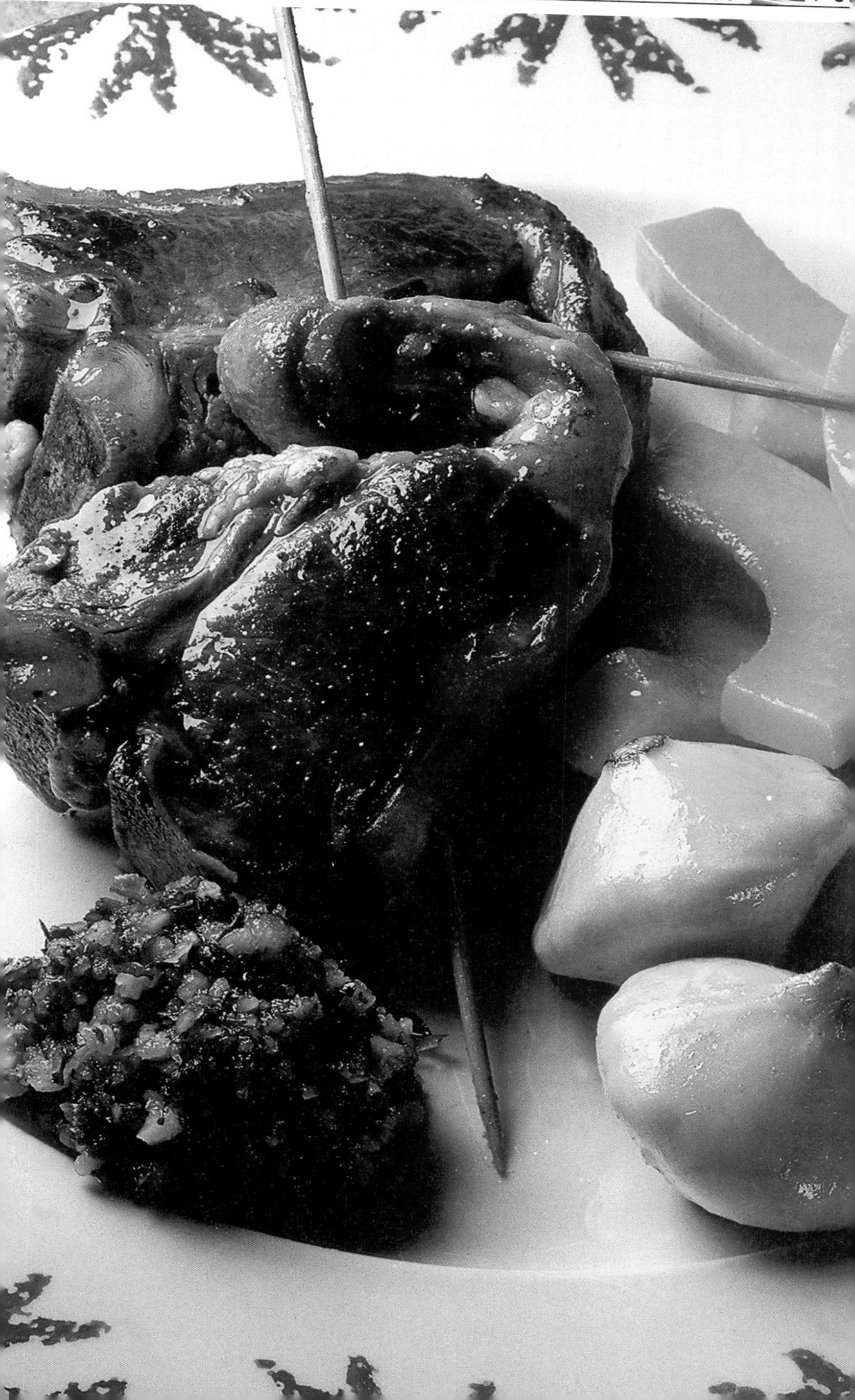

veal piccata

fruit salad
with lemon syrup

pears
with berry coulis

■□□ | Cooking time: 0 minute - Preparation time: 15 minutes

method

1. To make coulis, place blueberries, raspberries, orange juice and icing sugar in a blender or food processor (a), blend until smooth. Push mixture through a sieve (b) and discard pips. Spoon the coulis onto each serving plate.
2. Arrange pear halves and extra blueberries on the coulis.
3. Place 4 small droplets of cream on the coulis. Carefully pull a skewer through the coulis and through the center of each droplet without lifting the skewer (c).

ingredients

> 1/2 cup blueberries
> 1 cup raspberries
> 4 tablespoons freshly squeezed orange juice
> 2 tablespoons icing sugar
> 12 canned pear halves, drained
> 3/4 cup blueberries, extra
> 1/4 cup thickened cream

....
Serves 4

tip from the chef
This beautiful decoration is easy to achieve if coulis has the same consistency of cream.

a

b

c

berry compote

■□□ | Cooking time: 10 minutes - Preparation time: 5 minutes

ingredients

> **1 cup boysenberries or blackberries**
> **1 cup raspberries**
> **1/4 cup red wine**
> **3 tablespoons freshly squeezed lemon juice**
> **3 tablespoons sugar**
> **1 cup fresh strawberries, hulled and halved**
> **mint to garnish**

method

1. Place boysenberries or blackberries, raspberries, wine, lemon juice and sugar in a small saucepan over moderate heat, simmer gently until syrup begins to boil.
2. Remove berries from pan with a slotted spoon and set aside. Boil syrup for 5 minutes.
3. Add strawberries to the poached berries and divide between 4 serving glasses.
4. Cool syrup for 5 minutes, then pour over berries. Garnish with mint.

....
Serves 4

tip from the chef

When out of season, this recipe can be prepared using frozen red fruits.

index